500 words
Level 2

焦仲卿与刘兰芝

Zhongqing and Lanzhi, a Chinese Tragedy

刘菊 改编　范萍萍 翻译

MP3 Download Online

Sinolingua
华语教学出版社

First Edition 2016
Third Printing 2019

ISBN 978-7-5138-0976-4
Copyright 2016 by Sinolingua Co., Ltd
Published by Sinolingua Co., Ltd
24 Baiwanzhuang Street, Beijing 100037, China
Tel: (86) 10-68320585 68997826
Fax: (86) 10-68997826 68326333
http://www.sinolingua.com.cn
E-mail: hyjx@sinolingua.com.cn
Facebook: www.facebook.com/sinolingua
Printed by Beijing Jinghua Hucais Printing Co., Ltd

Printed in the People's Republic of China

编者的话

对于广大汉语学习者来说，要想快速提高汉语水平，扩大阅读量是很有必要的。"彩虹桥"汉语分级读物为汉语学习者提供了一系列有趣、有用的汉语阅读材料。本系列读物按照词汇量进行分级，并通过精彩的故事叙述，给读者带来了丰富有趣的阅读享受。本套读物主要有以下特点：

一、**分级精准，循序渐进**。我们参考了新汉语水平考试（HSK）词汇表（2012年修订版）、《汉语国际教育用音节汉字词汇等级划分（国家标准）》和《常用汉语1500高频词语表》等词汇分级标准，结合《欧洲语言教学与评估框架性共同标准》（CEFR），设计了一套适合汉语学习者的"彩虹桥"词汇分级标准。本系列读物分为7个级别（入门级*、1级、2级、3级、4级、5级、6级），供不同水平的汉语学习者选择，每个级别故事的生词数量不超过本级别对应词汇量的20%。随着级别的升高，故事的篇幅逐渐加长。本系列读物与HSK、CEFR的对应级别，各级词汇量以及每本书的字数详见下表。

---

* 入门级（Starter）在封底用 S 标识。

级别	入门级	1级	2级	3级	4级	5级	6级
对应级别	HSK1 CEFR A1	HSK1-2 CEFR A1-A2	HSK2-3 CEFR A2-B1	HSK3 CEFR A2-B1	HSK3-4 CEFR B1	HSK4 CEFR B1-B2	HSK5 CEFR B2-C1
词汇量	150	300	500	750	1 000	1 500	2 500
字数	1 000	2 500	5 000	7 500	10 000	15 000	25 000

二、**故事精彩，题材多样**。本套读物选材的标准就是"精彩"，所选的故事要么曲折离奇，要么感人至深，对读者构成奇妙的吸引力。选题广泛取材于中国的神话传说、民间故事、文学名著、名人传记和历史故事等，让汉语学习者在阅读中潜移默化地了解中国的文化和历史。

三、**结构合理，实用性强**。"彩虹桥"系列读物的每一本书中，除了中文故事正文之外，都配有主要人物的中英文介绍、生词英文注释及例句、故事正文的英文翻译、练习题以及生词表，方便读者阅读和理解故事内容，提升汉语阅读能力。练习题主要采用客观题，题型多样，难度适中，并附有参考答案，既可供汉语教师在课堂上教学使用，又可供汉语学习者进行自我水平检测。

如果您对本系列读物有什么想法，比如推荐精彩故事、提出改进意见等，请发邮件到 liuxiaolin@sinolingua.com.cn，与我们交流探讨。也可以关注我们的微信公众号 CHQRainbowBridge，随时与我们交流互动。同时，微信公众号会不定期发布有关"彩虹桥"的出版信息，以及汉语阅读、中国文化小知识等。

韩　颖　刘小琳

Preface

For students who study Chinese as a foreign language, it's crucial for them to enlarge the scope of their reading to improve their comprehension skills. The "Rainbow Bridge" Graded Chinese Reader series is designed to provide a collection of interesting and useful Chinese reading materials. This series grades each volume by its vocabulary level and brings the learners into every scene through vivid storytelling. The series has the following features:

I. A gradual approach by grading the volumes based on vocabulary levels. We have consulted the New HSK Vocabulary (2012 Revised Edition), the *Graded Chinese Syllables, Characters and Words for the Application of Teaching Chinese to the Speakers of Other Languages (National Standard)* and the 1500 Commonly Used High Frequency Chinese Vocabulary, along with the Common European Framework of Reference for Languages (CEFR) to design the "Rainbow Bridge" vocabulary grading standard. The series is divided into seven levels (Starter*, Level 1, Level 2, Level 3, Level 4, Level 5 and Level 6) for students at different stages in their Chinese education to choose from. For each level, new words are no more than 20% of the vocabulary amount as specified in the corresponding HSK and CEFR levels.

---

* Represented by "S" on the back cover.

As the levels progress, the passage length will in turn increase. The following table indicates the corresponding "Rainbow Bridge" level, HSK and CEFR levels, the vocabulary amount, and number of characters.

Level	Starter	1	2	3	4	5	6
HSK/ CEFR Level	HSK1 CEFR A1	HSK1-2 CEFR A1-A2	HSK2-3 CEFR A2-B1	HSK3 CEFR A2-B1	HSK3-4 CEFR B1	HSK4 CEFR B1-B2	HSK5 CEFR B2-C1
Vocabulary	150	300	500	750	1000	1500	2500
Characters	1000	2500	5000	7500	10,000	15,000	25,000

II. Intriguing stories on various themes. The series features engaging stories known for their twists and turns as well as deeply touching plots. The readers will find it a joyful experience to read the stories. The topics are selected from Chinese mythology, legends, folklore, literary classics, biographies of renowned people and historical tales. Such widely ranged topics would exert an invisible, yet formative, influence on readers' understanding of Chinese culture and history.

III. Reasonably structured and easy to use. For each volume of the "Rainbow Bridge" series, apart from a Chinese story, we also provide an introduction to the main characters in Chinese and English, new words with English explanations and sample sentences, and an English translation of the story, followed by comprehension exercises and a vocabulary list to help users read and understand the story and improve their Chinese reading skills. The exercises are mainly presented as objective questions that take on various forms with moderate difficulty. Moreover, keys to the exercises are also provided. The series can be used by teachers in class or by students for self-study.

If you have any questions, comments or suggestions about the series, please email us at liuxiaolin@sinolingua.com.cn. You can also exchange ideas with us via our WeChat account: CHQRainbowBridge. This account will provide updates on the series along with Chinese reading materials and cultural tips.

Han Ying and Liu Xiaolin

主要人物
Main Characters of the Story

刘兰芝 (Liú Lánzhī)：焦仲卿的妻子，漂亮可爱又有才能。
Liu Lanzhi: The pretty and talented wife of Jiao Zhongqing.

焦仲卿 (Jiāo Zhòngqīng)：刘兰芝的丈夫，年轻上进的小官员。
Jiao Zhongqing: A young and ambitious petty official, husband of Liu Lanzhi.

焦母 (Jiāo mǔ)：性格暴躁，非常讨厌刘兰芝。
Mother of Jiao Zhongqing: She is hot-tempered and dislikes Liu Lanzhi very much.

刘兄 (Liú xiōng)：趋炎附势，冷酷无情。
Brother of Liu Lanzhi: A snobbish and cold-hearted person.

刘母 (Liú mǔ)：跟刘兰芝的哥哥住在一起，很爱女儿刘兰芝。
Mother of Liu Lanzhi: She lives with her son and loves her daughter dearly.

中文故事

焦仲卿与刘兰芝

　　一千多年前，中国有一个漂亮、可爱的小女孩儿，她的名字叫刘兰芝。远近的人们都认为她像花儿一样美。人们都很喜欢刘兰芝。他们常常说："我要是有个像刘兰芝这么漂亮的女儿就好了！"

时间像水一样一天天过去，<u>刘兰芝</u>也从一个小女孩儿长成了少女。这时的<u>刘兰芝</u>不只漂亮可爱，还非常有才能。她在十三四岁时就学会了自己动手做衣服。在她十五岁时，父母找人教她学习音乐，她学得很认真。十六岁时，她读书就已经读得很好了，连她的哥哥都比不过她。

① 娶 (qǔ) *v.*
(of men) marry
e.g., 他娶了一个漂亮的女孩子。

② 媒人 (méirén) *n.*
matchmaker
e.g., 她是我们两个的媒人。
In ancient China, all marriages must start with matchmakers. A man and a woman could get married only after the matchmaking activities. The matchmakers could proactively act as the go-between, or could be entrusted by the man's family. An old Chinese saying "(marriage must be) decided by the parents and arranged by the matchmakers" was the true reflection of the time.

③ 嫁 (jià) *v.* (of women) marry
e.g., 她嫁给了自己喜欢的人。

人们更喜欢刘兰芝了。他们常常说："我要是有个像刘兰芝这么有才能的女儿就好了！"

又一年飞快地过去了，刘兰芝十七岁了。只要是听过刘兰芝名字的青年男子，都很想娶①刘兰芝为妻子。他们都让父母找了媒人②，请媒人去问刘兰芝愿不愿意嫁③给自己。这其中就有焦仲卿。

刘兰芝的父母见每天都有媒人到来，非常高兴。他们想："有这么多人喜欢我们的女儿，女儿应该很快就可以嫁出去了！我们要好好帮女儿找个好人家。"每次有媒人来，他们都会很认真地问媒人："你

介绍的这个男子个子高不高?长得怎么样?心眼儿好不好?家庭情况怎么样?"媒人一一回答之后,他们还会问个不停。

后来,刘兰芝的父母注意到了年轻、上进的焦仲卿。正好焦仲卿家请的媒人也到了刘家。媒人告诉刘兰芝的父母:"焦仲卿

① 官员 (guānyuán) n. official
e.g., 官员要多为人们做好事。

② 太守 (tàishǒu) n. prefect, a position in ancient China equivalent to current provincial governor.
e.g., 太守是中国古代相当于省长的大官。

个子很高,长得也很精神,和兰芝算是天生一对。他是个小官员①,跟着太守②办事。人很好,一定会好好对兰芝的。他的家庭情况也不错,虽然他的父亲不在了,但他的母亲和妹妹人很好,兰芝嫁过去之后会过得很幸福的!"

刘兰芝的父母对焦仲卿非常满意,于是便放心地

把女儿嫁给了他。就这样，刘兰芝在十七岁这一年嫁给了焦仲卿，成了他的妻子。结婚以后，焦仲卿对刘兰芝非常好，而且焦仲卿也喜欢音乐，喜欢看书。虽然焦仲卿的工作很忙，在家的时间很少，但是他回家后，都会帮刘兰芝干活儿。刘兰芝也很爱焦仲

卿，焦仲卿在家的时候，她就为他唱歌、跳舞。她想："能和自己爱的人在一起，我真的很幸福！"

只是，让刘兰芝没想到的是，焦仲卿的母亲非常不喜欢她。焦仲卿结婚后，老是和刘兰芝在一起，和母亲在一起的时间就少了。刘兰芝在刘家很少干活儿，到了焦家以后，她努力学习做家务，但做得不够好，这让焦仲卿的母亲很不高兴。每天一大早，她就对刘兰芝说："都几点了，还不快干活儿去！"晚上很晚了，她也不让刘兰芝去休息，而是对她说："这才几点，你就想去睡觉了？"她还常常生气地对刘兰芝

说:"你怎么干活儿这么慢,还想不想吃饭了?"刘兰芝每天都忙着干活儿,再也不能像在刘家那样,做自己喜欢做的事,看自己喜欢看的书了。

一开始,刘兰芝很难过,但是她对自己说:"一切都会好起来的!只要我好好努力,她一定会慢慢

① 笨 (bèn) *adj.*
stupid
e.g., 他太笨了，那么简单的题都不会做。

② 赶 (gǎn) *v.*
drive away
e.g., 他把那只猫赶出去了。

喜欢我的！"没想到，两年过去了，她每天都忙着干活儿，焦仲卿的母亲对她还是很不满，常常对她说："你怎么这么笨①？过两天我就让我儿子把你赶②回刘家去！"

刘兰芝越来越不快乐了。她努力干活儿，却总是难以让焦仲卿的母亲满意，她也不知道怎么才能让焦仲卿的母亲喜欢自己。焦仲卿工作很忙，很少在家，也就没发现妻子的不开心。他每次回到家，都会问自己的妻子最近过得好不好。这时，刘兰芝很想把自己的心事告诉丈夫焦仲卿。可是为了不让丈夫担心，她总是对他说：

"我很好,你就放心吧!"

焦仲卿的母亲越来越不喜欢刘兰芝,就想把她赶走。有一次,焦仲卿刚回到家,他的母亲便把他叫了过去,冷冷地说:"刘兰芝已经嫁到我们家两三年了,她常常想做什么就做什么,想说什么就说什么,一点儿规矩①都没有。让她做点儿家务吧,她也不好好干。最重要的是,我就你

① 规矩 (guīju) n. (good) manners
e.g., 他是个没有规矩的小孩儿。

① 休 (xiū) v. divorce (one's wife)
e.g., 在中国古代，男人可以休妻。
It referred to the situation in ancient China when a husband sent his wife back to her maiden home and cut off their relationship. Chinese women in the past must be faithful to their husbands unto death, and they did not have the right to ask for a divorce. Only a man had the right to drive his wife away back to her family. This is called 休妻 (divorce one's wife).

② 怪 (guài) v. blame
e.g., 这件事你只能怪你自己。

③ 脾气 (píqi) n. temper
e.g., 他的脾气很不好。

这么一个儿子，这么长时间她都没能给你生个孩子。[1] 让她在我们家还有什么用？你还是把她休①了吧！"

焦仲卿一听，连忙对母亲说："我跟兰芝结婚这几年来，她对家人一直很好，哪里能说休就休呢？生孩子这件事情，不怪②兰芝。是我自己工作太忙，在家的时间太少了。我们会有孩子的。她在刘家的时候，她的家人很爱她，所以她有点小脾气③也没什么。而且她每天从早忙到晚，母亲您怎么能说她不好好干活儿呢？"

焦仲卿的母亲见焦仲卿为刘兰芝说话，便大声说："太不像话了！你连我的话都不听了吗？不管你怎么说，我都不喜欢她。我们邻居①家有个美人儿，我觉得很不错。只要你把刘兰芝休了，我就请媒人去她家，让她嫁给你。"

焦仲卿生气地对母亲说："母亲您别说了！就算您把兰芝赶走了，我也不会再娶其他人的！"焦仲

① 邻居 (línjū) n. neighbor
e.g., 他的邻居很喜欢猫。

① 不孝 (búxiào) v. be unfilial
e.g., 他真是不孝，让老母亲自己一个人住在乡下。

② 接 (jiē) v. pick up
e.g., 他去接他的女儿去了。

卿的母亲一听，心里的火一下子被点着了，她大声说："你不要再说了！就这么决定了！你要是不同意，那就是不孝！①"[2] 焦仲卿还想再说些什么，母亲已经回她自己的房间去了。

刘兰芝见焦仲卿很不开心，马上就明白了一切。焦仲卿哭着对刘兰芝说："我母亲想让我休了你。我很爱你，怎么可能会跟你分开呢？只是我现在工作有点儿忙，马上就又要去太守那里办事去了。我先把你送回你家。等我忙完了，就去接②你回家。你看怎么样？"

刘兰芝心里想："这一天还是到来了！"她难过

地对丈夫说:"你们想要把我赶走的话,那就赶吧!在焦家的这几年,我一直忙来忙去,却还是得不到你母亲的喜欢。她怎么又会同意让你把我接回来呢?只怕是这次分开了,我们就再也不能见面了!我的那些衣服,我就不带回刘家去了。希望你看到它们的时候,还能想起我。"两个人说着说着就一起哭了起来,像是永远也不能再见面了一样。

第二天,刘兰芝去了焦仲卿的母亲和妹妹的房间,向她们一一道别。刘兰芝对焦仲卿的妹妹说:"刚来到焦家时,你还是个可爱的小女孩儿。而现在,

你都已经长成一个漂亮的少女了。这几年来，我们常常一起做伴。现在，我要离开焦家了，以后就不能和你做伴了。真是让人心痛啊！希望你不要忘记我。"焦仲卿的妹妹很难过，但是她也没有办法。

为了能让焦仲卿永远记住自己，刘兰芝一大早就起来打扮①了。她把自己打扮得很美，像是画儿里才有的美人儿一样。焦仲卿看着眼前漂亮的妻子，认真地说："我说过我会永远和你在一起，所以我一定不会对不起你的。等我忙完工作上的事情，马上就去刘家接你回来。"

刘兰芝听了之后很感

① 打扮 (dǎban) v.
dress up
e.g., 她把女儿打扮得很漂亮。

动,她对焦仲卿说:"只要你还像以前一样爱我,我就很开心了。你可要早点儿来接我,不要忘记了。我怕在家住的时间长了,哥哥有可能会让我嫁给其他人。"焦仲卿点了点头。

刘兰芝的母亲见刘兰芝被焦仲卿送回了刘家,很

不高兴。她问刘兰芝："你怎么回来了？你是不是做错了什么，才让人家给赶回来了？"刘兰芝不知道该怎么回答，她只能说："我真的没有做错什么。"[3]

很多大官听说漂亮又有才能的刘兰芝被休回了刘家，都非常高兴。他们找了媒人去刘家，去问刘兰

① 有钱有势 (yǒu qián yǒu shì) rich and powerful
e.g., 他家有钱有势。

② 礼物 (lǐwù) *n.* gift
e.g., 我送你一个礼物吧！

芝愿不愿意嫁给自己的儿子。有钱有势①的太守想让刘兰芝嫁给自己的第五个儿子，还让媒人给刘家送了很多礼物②。

刘兰芝的母亲见媒人一个个地来刘家，心里想："她离开了焦家也好，看样子这次她会嫁到更好的人家呢。"她把很多官员请媒人来提亲的事情告诉了刘兰芝，以为她听了之后会很开心。没想到刘兰芝却说："我不愿意嫁给他们。我离开焦家时，仲卿再三告诉我，他一忙完工作，就会来接我回去的。所以我要等着他。如果再有媒人来，你就把他们都打发走吧。"刘兰芝的母亲

见刘兰芝还在等着焦仲卿，就只好把所有的媒人都送走了。

刘兰芝的哥哥听说刘兰芝不愿意嫁给太守的儿子，非常不高兴。他对妹妹说："你被焦家赶出来后，一直住在我家。我是你哥哥，你吃我的、喝我的，我都没话说。不过你也应该好好想想，以后该怎么办呢？你最后还是要嫁人的。太守的儿子有钱有势，比焦仲卿那个小官员不知道好多少。你不嫁给他，还想嫁给谁呢？难不成你要一个人生活到老吗？"[4]

刘兰芝想："我离开焦家这么长时间了,丈夫还没有来接我回去。回焦家应该是没什么可能了。我已经在哥哥家住了这么长时间,再住下去是有点儿不好意思。我只能一切都听哥哥的了。"想到这里,刘兰芝对哥哥说："你想怎么办,就怎么办吧。我都听你的。"哥哥一听,非常高兴,说："这才是我的好妹妹。我马上就去准备你和太守儿子结婚的事情。"

太守听说刘兰芝同意嫁给自己的儿子了,非常开心。他告诉了刘兰芝的哥哥娶刘兰芝的日子,还送了很多很多的礼物到刘家,有好马好车,也有山

③ 山珍海味
(shānzhēn-hǎiwèi)
idiom delicacies of every kind
e.g., 不是每个人都想要吃山珍海味。

珍海味①。太守一家很开心，刘兰芝的母亲和哥哥也很开心，只有刘兰芝自己不开心。

结婚的日子马上就要到了，刘兰芝还没开始打扮自己。她坐在自己的房间里，一个人哭啊哭，从白天哭到晚上，又从月亮出

来哭到月亮下去。她问自己:"我到底①做错了什么,上天才会这么对我,让我嫁给自己不爱的人。"

焦仲卿正在太守那里办事,听说太守的第五个儿子要娶刘兰芝,马上请假回家了。他骑②着马去了刘兰芝哥哥家。还没到刘兰芝哥哥家,马就开始叫起来,像是知道焦仲卿和刘

① 到底 (dàodǐ) adv. on earth
e.g., 你到底在想什么啊?

② 骑 (qí) v. ride
e.g., 他骑着马去了那里。

兰芝都很难过一样。刘兰芝听到了马的叫声,知道丈夫到了;她又高兴又难过。高兴的是,自己终于可以见到丈夫了;难过的是,自己马上要嫁给别人了。

刘兰芝对焦仲卿说:"我回到刘家之后,有很多人找媒人到我家来,问我愿不愿意嫁给他们。母亲希望

我能早早地嫁出去,哥哥一次次地来劝①我嫁给太守的儿子。我住在哥哥家,只能一切都听哥哥的。哥哥让我嫁给谁,我只能嫁给谁。我爱你,却要嫁给别人,我真的很难过。"

焦仲卿对刘兰芝说:"你马上就要嫁到有钱有势的太守家了,有什么好难过的?我应该祝贺②你才是。我们以前说好的,要永远在一起。而现在,你却要离开我了。我一个人活着也没有什么意义③了。你过你的幸福生活去吧,我要离开这个世界了!"

刘兰芝听到这里,生气地说:"你怎么能这么说呢?能和你在一起,是我

① 劝 (quàn) v. persuade
e.g., 他劝她离开那里。

② 祝贺 (zhùhè) v. congratulate
e.g., 祝贺你拿到了第一名。

③ 意义 (yìyì) n. meaning
e.g., 这是一件很有意义的事。

① 心愿 (xīnyuàn) n. wish
e.g., 他的心愿是能去国外走走。

这一生最大的心愿①。和你在一起,我才会快乐,你也才会快乐。你母亲让你休了我,你很难过。可是我母亲和哥哥让我嫁给太守的儿子,我也很难过啊!看来我们活着是不可能在一起了。如果活着不能在一起,那就让我们死在一起吧！只要你不害怕①，我也没什么好害怕的！"焦仲卿听妻子说完，大哭起来。他明白，他不可能不听他母亲的话，把刘兰芝带回家；也不可能带刘兰芝一起走，离开他的母亲，因为这么做是"不孝"。在他的心里，只

① 害怕 (hàipà) v.
fear
e.g., 他很害怕那只猫。

① 死亡 (sǐwáng) *n.* death
e.g., 没有人不害怕死亡。

② 健康 (jiànkāng) *adj.* healthy
e.g., 他很老了,却还很健康。

要他活着,他就不能做一个"不孝"的人。但是他也不能没有刘兰芝。于是他看着她的眼睛,对她说:"好,就这么办了!谁也别想把我们分开!就算是死亡①,也不能把我们分开!"

就这样,焦仲卿哭着离开刘兰芝,回家去了。他找到母亲,对她说:"今天的风好大,天好冷。我的心情却比这天气还要差。和兰芝分开之后,我总是觉得我的精神不怎么好,只怕是我将要离开这个世界了。如果儿子我不在您旁边了,母亲您也不要为我难过,一定要开心、健康②地生活下去。"

焦仲卿的母亲听到这

里哭了起来,她对儿子说:"刘兰芝又没有什么特别的地方,你为什么要为了她想不开呢?你又年轻又上进,娶个又漂亮又有才能的女子还不是很容易的事情吗?我们邻居家有个美人儿,人人都很喜欢她。我明天去找媒人去她家,

她一定会同意嫁给你的。你可不要想不开啊!"

焦仲卿离开母亲,来到他和妻子刘兰芝住的房间。房间里只有他一个人,但是他记得自己和妻子在一起所有的快乐。他记得她第一次来到自己家时,像小孩子一样高兴;他记得她一边做家务一边笑得

很开心；他记得她一边跟他说话，一边把自己打扮得像画儿里的美人儿一样……他们曾经①那么幸福地生活在一起，最后却还是不得不分开。想到这里，他又一次哭了起来。

刘兰芝出嫁的前一天，她的母亲和哥哥都很开心，她的脸上却没有一点儿开心的样子，好像结婚只是别人的事情一样。月亮出来了，晚上到来了，人们都准备休息了。刘兰芝一个人来到了院子②里的水塘③旁边，她在那里坐了一会儿，见旁边没有人，便一下子跳了下去。

很快，焦仲卿便听说了刘兰芝死去的事情。他知

① 曾经 (céngjīng) *adv.* once
e.g., 我曾经去过那里。

② 院子 (yuànzi) *n.* courtyard
e.g., 她家的院子很大。

③ 水塘 (shuǐtáng) *n.* pool
e.g., 那儿有一个大水塘。

① 上吊 (shàngdiào)
v. hang oneself
e.g., 有个人上吊了。

道这个世界上再也没有刘兰芝这个人了,她已经为了爱情而选择了死亡。他在院子里的大树下走来走去,在心里说着:"兰芝,你等着我,我现在就去找你。我们很快就又可以在一起了!"随后,他在树上上吊①了。

焦仲卿和刘兰芝死后，他们的家人才明白他们爱得有多深①。焦仲卿的母亲觉得自己很对不起这一对小夫妻②。就是因为她把刘兰芝赶回刘家，才让二人不得不分开。刘兰芝的哥哥也觉得自己对不起妹妹。也正是因为他让兰芝嫁给不喜欢的人，才让她对生活失去③了希望。正是因为他们的过错，才使得这对小夫妻不得不选择了一起走向死亡。

焦、刘两家把焦仲卿和刘兰芝合葬④在一座山的旁边，又在二人的墓地⑤旁边种了很多树。树越长越大，有两只小鸟⑥飞来住在里面。在白天的阳光里，在

① 深 (shēn) *adj.* deep
e.g., 那边的水很深。

② 夫妻 (fūqī) *n.* husband and wife, couple
e.g., 那一对夫妻人很好。

③ 失去 (shīqù) *v.* lose
e.g., 他说他不能失去她。

④ 合葬 (hézàng) *v.* bury in one grave
e.g., 他们家人把他们两个合葬在了一起。

⑤ 墓地 (mùdì) *n.* grave
e.g., 墓地旁边有很多树。

⑥ 小鸟 (xiǎo niǎo) *n.* little bird
e.g., 小鸟正在树上唱歌。

① 强迫 (qiǎngpò) v. force, compel
e.g., 你不要强迫他去那里。

晚上的小雨里，它们一起飞来飞去，一起唱歌、跳舞，每天叫个不停，快乐地生活着。

年长的老人经过这里，会告诉年轻的人们："等你们的孩子长大了，一定不要强迫①自己的孩子跟不爱的人在一起，也不要强迫他们跟自己爱的人分开。焦仲卿和刘兰芝就是因为受到家人强迫，才为爱去死的，这里就是他们的墓地。不过他们并没有真正死去，而是变成了两只快乐的小鸟，永远幸福地生活在了一起。他们的生命是短暂①的，而爱却是永恒②的。"

① 短暂 (duǎnzàn)
adj. brief, transient
e.g., 虽然在那儿的时间很短暂，他还是学到了很多东西。

② 永恒 (yǒnghéng)
adj. eternal
e.g., 没有什么东西是永恒不变的。

[1] 在中国古代，家族的延续被认为是婚姻最重要的目的，所谓"不孝有三，无后为大"，因此，妻子无法生出子女来便是天大的罪过，丈夫及其家族便可以要求休妻。
In ancient China, the most important purpose of marriage was to continue the family line. Just as the saying goes, there are three ways of being an unfilial son, the most serious is to have no heir. If a wife can't give birth to children, she would be considered to be guilty and her husband may divorce her.

[2] 中国封建时代标榜"孝道"，父母永远都是对的，子女要听父母的话，娶谁休谁当然得由父母说了算。汉朝法律还规定，不孝是死罪。在"孝道"的枷锁之下，仲卿对母亲的不近情理也只能惟命是从。

In feudal times, filial piety was ranked high in China: Parents were always right, sons and daughters must listen to their parents all the time. Thus, parents naturally decided for their children whom to marry and divorce. The law of the Han Dynasty (206 BC-220 AD) even stipulated that a person unfilial to his or her parents could be sentenced to death. Jiao had no choice but to agree to his mother's arrangement under such requirements.

[3] 中国古代男尊女卑，女人是男人的附庸，女人出嫁之后被夫家休弃回到娘家，是很丢脸的事情。

In ancient China, women were inferior to men, and wives were supposed to be dependents of their husbands. It was a shameful thing for a woman to be divorced and sent back to her maiden family.

[4] 在中国古代封建社会，女人出嫁后就是丈夫家的人，除了嫁人时从娘家带走的嫁妆，不再继承娘家的财产。刘兰芝被休后，没有任何经济来源，在娘家的地位很低。而刘兰芝的哥哥作为刘家的成年男人，掌握一家经济来源，是刘家的一家之主。

In feudal China, a married woman became a member of her husband's family. She could no longer inherit property from her parents except the dowry. After Liu's divorce, she had no financial income and had a very low status in her maiden family. As the only adult man in the Liu family, her brother was the head of the family who controlled the economic resources.

> **English Version**

Zhongqing and Lanzhi, a Chinese Tragedy

Around a thousand years ago, there was a cute little girl named Liu Lanzhi in China. People from far and near agreed that she was as beautiful as a flower. They adored her and would often say, "If only I had a daughter as beautiful as her."

Time went by quickly. Lanzhi grew into a teenager. Besides beauty and charm, she was also blessed with many talents. At around 13 or 14, she learned to make clothes by herself. At 15, she began to study music with a teacher her parents picked out. At 16, she could read better than her elder brother. She became more and more adorable. People often said, "If only I had a daughter as versatile as her."

Another year passed quickly. Lanzhi turned 17. Every young man who had heard about Lanzhi wanted to marry her. They asked their parents to send matchmakers to Lanzhi's home with their marriage proposals. Jiao Zhongqing was one of them.

Lanzhi's parents were delighted to see the coming of matchmakers every day. They thought, "Now that so many men are fond of our daughter, she could get married soon. We shall pick a good family for her." Whenever the matchmakers came, they would earnestly ask, "Is the man tall? What does he look like? Is he kind-hearted? What is his family like?" After the matchmakers had answered these questions, Lanzhi's parents would ask some more.

Then young and ambitious Jiao Zhongqing caught the attention of Lanzhi's parents. At the request of Zhongqing's family, the matchmaker came to the Lanzhi family just in time, and she said, "Zhongqing is tall and handsome. He and Lanzhi will make a perfect couple. As a petty official, he is serving the governor of the prefecture. He will treat Lanzhi well since he is a very nice man. His father has passed away. His mother and sister are both very kind. Lanzhi will live a happy life after marriage."

Lanzhi's parents were satisfied with Zhongqing and agreed to the marriage. Lanzhi was then married to Zhongqing at the age of 17. After marriage, Zhongqing was very nice to Lanzhi. Besides, he also loved music and reading. Although he was busy with work and was seldom at home, he would help his wife with housework after work. Lanzhi loved Zhongqing, too. When her husband was home, she would sing and dance for him. Lanzhi thought to herself, "I am really happy to be with my loved one."

To Lanzhi's dismay, Zhongqing's mother did not like her a bit. Zhongqing always stayed with Lanzhi after marriage and had little time for his mother. Lanzhi seldom did housework at home. After marriage she tried hard to learn, but she still didn't do well enough, which made her mother-in-law very unhappy. In the early morning every day, Zhongqing's mother would shout at Lanzhi, "It's getting late! Go do your work!" Late in the evening, she wouldn't let Lanzhi go to bed, saying, "It's still very early, and you're already thinking of going to bed?" Often she would scold Lanzhi angrily, "Why are you so inefficient? Don't you want to eat dinner?" Every day, Lanzhi was busy with lots of housework and could no longer do what she liked and read her favorite books as she used to in her parents' home.

At the beginning, Lanzhi was very upset, but she said to herself,

"Everything will be okay with my effort. I will work hard, and she will surely grow to like me." Unfortunately, after two years of endless work, Zhongqing's mother was still unsatisfied with Lanzhi and often said to her, "How stupid you are! I will ask my son to kick you back to your parents' home soon."

Lanzhi grew more and more depressed. She worked hard but that was still far from satisfactory to Zhongqing's mother. She did not know how to make her mother-in-law like her. Zhongqing was busy with work and was seldom at home, so he did not know that his wife was unhappy. When he got home, he would ask how she was doing. Lanzhi wanted to tell him what was on her mind, but she did not want him to worry about her and so she always answered, "I'm fine. Don't worry."

Zhongqing's mother's dislike of Lanzhi grew stronger and stronger. She wanted to drive her away even more. One day, when Zhongqing got home, his mother called him over and said coldly, "Liu Lanzhi has come to our home for over two years now. She often does whatever she likes and says whatever she wants. She has no manners. When I asked her to do some work, she didn't put her mind to it. Above all, you are my only son and she has not yet given birth to a child for such a long time. What is she staying here for? You have to kick her out."

Hearing this, Zhongqing responded quickly, "Since we were married, she has been good to everyone these years. How can I kick her out? As for the child, it's not her fault. I have been too busy with my work and have spent too little time at home. We shall have a baby. It is true that she has a small temper since she was a little spoiled back in her parents' family. However, she has been working so hard here all these years, getting up early and going to bed late. Why did you say she didn't put her mind to the work?"

Seeing that her son was taking Lanzhi's side, Zhongqing's mother yelled, "What a shame! Are you trying to disobey me? Whatever you say, I won't like her. Our neighbor has a pretty girl and I like her very much. If you divorce Liu Lanzhi, I will find a matchmaker to ask the girl to marry you."

Zhongqing got angry, "Mother, please don't talk about this anymore. Even if you drive Lanzhi away, I won't marry another woman." Hearing his words, Zhongqing's mother grew very angry, "Don't say anything anymore. It's settled. If you object to my proposal, you'll be unfilial." Zhongqing wanted to argue, but his mother had gone back to her own room.

Noticing that Zhongqing was upset, Lanzhi immediately understood what was wrong. Zhongqing wept, "My mother wants me to divorce you. I love you so much. How can I part with you? Now, I am really busy at work and have to go back to get something done for the governor of the prefecture right away. Can I send you back to your home now and pick you up as soon as I am done with my work?"

Lanzhi thought to herself, "The day has finally come." She said sadly, "If you want me to go, I will go. I have been working so hard these years but still can't win your mother's heart. How will she approve of the idea of taking me back? I am afraid we shall never see each other again if we are separated this time. As for my clothes, I won't take them with me. I hope they will remind you of me after I'm gone." After these words, the two burst into tears as if they would never see each other again.

The next day, Lanzhi went to the room of Zhongqing's mother and sister to bid farewell. Lanzhi said to Zhongqing's sister,

"When I got here, you were a lovely little girl. Now you have grown into a pretty young lady. We often stayed together during these years. Now I am leaving and can't stay with you anymore. What a pity! I hope you will never forget me." Zhongqing's sister was very sad, but she couldn't do anything.

On the day of her departure, Lanzhi got up very early to dress herself up. She wished that Zhongqing would remember her forever. After dressing up, Lanzhi looked as beautiful as a beauty in the painting. Zhongqing looked at his pretty wife and said to her earnestly, "I have said I will stay with you forever, and I will surely keep my words. As soon as I finish my work at hand, I will get you back right away."

Lanzhi was deeply moved, "As long as you love me like before, I will be happy. Don't forget to pick me up early. I am afraid my brother will ask me to marry other men if I stay with them for too long." Zhongqing nodded.

Lanzhi's mother was unhappy to see her return. She asked her daughter, "Why have you come back? Is it because you did something wrong?" Lanzhi did not know how to respond, she only said, "I did nothing wrong."

Many high-ranking officials were glad to learn that the pretty and talented Lanzhi had returned home. They immediately sent matchmakers to her home to propose marriage for their sons. The governor of the prefecture, who was rich and powerful, sent many gifts to Lanzhi's family through a matchmaker to ask Lanzhi to marry his fifth son.

Lanzhi's mother saw the matchmakers file in, and thought, "Maybe it is a good thing for her to leave Zhongqing. She can choose a better husband this time." She told Lanzhi about the matchmakers sent by the officials, believing that her daughter would be happy to hear it. Unexpectedly, Lanzhi said, "I won't marry any of them. When I left, Zhongqing repeatedly told me that he would come back for me as soon as he finished his work. I will wait for him. If matchmakers come, tell them to leave." Lanzhi's mother knew she was still waiting for Zhongqing and had to ask all the matchmakers to leave.

Lanzhi's brother was unhappy to learn that Lanzhi didn't agree to marry the son of the governor. He said to her, "After you were driven out of Zhongqing's family, you have been living in my home. I have no complaints when you ate my food and drank my water, as I am your brother. But you should think about your future. What will you do with yourself? You will have to marry someone. The governor's son is rich and powerful, much better than Jiao Zhongqing, who is just a petty official. Who do you want to marry if not him? Will you stay single for the rest of your life?"

Lanzhi thought to herself, "It's been a long time since I left Zhongqing's family. My husband still hasn't come for me. It seems there is no possibility for me to go back. I have lived in my brother's home for a long time. It will be a shame for me to live here any longer. I'd better listen to my brother." With that in mind, Lanzhi said to her brother, "Do what you want to do. I will obey you." Her brother was delighted, "There you go, my good sister. I will prepare for your marriage with the governor's son right away."

The governor was very happy to hear that Lanzhi had agreed to marry his son. He set the marriage date and informed Lanzhi's brother. He also sent many gifts to the Lanzhi family including fine horses and a carriage along with delicacies of all kinds. The governor's family was pleased, as was Lanzhi's mother and brother. Only Lanzhi herself was unhappy.

The wedding date was approaching and Lanzhi was still not ready to dress herself up. Instead, she sat in her room crying from day to night and until the moon rose and set. She asked herself, "What have I done wrong? Why does heaven treat me like this—marry someone I don't love?"

Zhongqing was working for the governor when he heard that the fifth son of the governor would marry Lanzhi. He asked for a leave right away and rode to the house of Lanzhi's brother. The horse began to neigh long before they reached Lanzhi's house as if it knew Zhongqing and Lanzhi were both sad. Hearing the neigh of the horse, Lanzhi knew her husband was coming. She was both happy and sad. She was happy because she would finally see her husband; she was sad because she would soon get married to another man.

Lanzhi said to Zhongqing, "After I got home, a lot of matchmakers came with marriage proposals. My mother wished I could get remarried as soon as possible, and my brother repeatedly tried to persuade me to marry the son of the governor. Now I'm living in my brother's home and have to obey him. My brother decided whom I shall marry. I love you, but I have to marry another man. I am really sad."

Zhongqing said to Lanzhi, "You don't have to feel sad. You're about to marry into the governor's family! I should congratulate you. We had promised to stay together forever. Now you are leaving me. It's meaningless for me to live on by myself. Go ahead with your happy life. I will say goodbye to this world."

Hearing that, Lanzhi got angry, "How can you say that? My

biggest wish is to live happily with you. I only feel happy when I'm with you. And you are happy with me, too. You are sad to divorce me in compliance with your mother's will. I am also sad to marry the son of the governor in compliance with my mother and brother's will. It seems that we are not destined to be together when we're alive. Then let's die together. If you are not afraid, neither am I." Zhongqing burst into tears at Lanzhi's words. He knew he could not disobey his mother and bring Lanzhi home, nor could he leave his mother to run away with Lanzhi, as that would make him an unfilial son. He could never allow himself to be unfilial. However, he also could not live happily without Lanzhi. Looking into her eyes, he said, "Okay, let's do it. Nothing can separate us, even death."

In tears, Zhongqing parted with Lanzhi and went home. He told his mother, "It's so windy and cold today. I am feeling worse than the weather. I have been depressed since my departure with Lanzhi. I am afraid I will leave this world soon. When I am not around, don't worry about me. Please live a happy and healthy life."

Zhongqing's mother cried at his words, "What's so special about Lanzhi! Why do you have to do silly things because of her? You are young and promising. Isn't it easy to marry another pretty and talented girl? Our neighbor's girl is a beauty and everyone likes her. Tomorrow, I will send a matchmaker to her family. She will surely agree to our proposal. Please don't do silly things."

Leaving his mother, Zhongqing entered the room in which Lanzhi used to live with him. He felt lonely, but remembered all the happiness they had together: she was as happy as a little child when she first came to his family; she laughed happily while doing housework; she could dress herself up like the beauty in the painting while chatting with him… They had been so happy together, but now they had to part with each other. Thinking of this, he began to wail again.

On the day before Lanzhi's wedding, her mother and brother were very happy, but she showed no sign of happiness as if it was not her who was getting married. The moon had come out, night fell, and people were getting ready for rest. Lanzhi went out to the courtyard and sat beside the pool for a while. Seeing that nobody was around, she jumped into the pool.

Very soon Zhongqing heard about Lanzhi's death. He knew that Lanzhi was no longer living in this world—she chose death for love. He walked up and down under a big tree in the courtyard and murmured in his heart, "Lanzhi, wait for me. Now I am going to find you, then we can be together soon." Then he hung himself on the tree.

Only after Zhongqing and Lanzhi committed suicide did their families realize how deeply they had been in love with each other. Zhongqing's mother regretted what she had done to the young couple. It was she who had driven Lanzhi back to her maiden home and made the loved ones part with each other. Lanzhi's brother also felt sorry for his sister because he forced her to marry a man she didn't love and thus made her lose hope in life. Because of their faults, the couple had no choice but to die together.

The two families buried Zhongqing and Lanzhi together beside a mountain and planted many trees near their grave. As the trees grew bigger and bigger, two birds came to live in the trees, chirping in the sunshine during the daytime or in the drizzle of the evenings. Every day, they flew here and there together, singing and dancing happily.

When old people passed by, they would tell the youngsters, "When your children grow up, don't ever force them to marry someone they don't love, or force anyone to part with their loved ones. Zhongqing and Lanzhi committed suicide for love due to the pressure from their families. Here is their grave. However, they haven't really died; they became two joyous birds, living together in happiness forever. Their lives may have been short, but their love is eternal."

练习题 Reading exercises

一、选择题。 Choose the correct answer.

1. 焦仲卿是一个什么人?（　　）

    A. 媒人　　　B. 小官员　　C. 太守　　D. 老师

2. 刘兰芝在她多大的时候嫁给了焦仲卿?（　　）

    A. 十五岁　　B. 十六岁　　C. 十七岁　　D. 十八岁

3. 刘兰芝和焦仲卿结婚几年了?（　　）

    A 半年　　　B. 一年　　　C. 两三年　　D. 四五年

4. 谁不喜欢刘兰芝?（　　）

    A. 刘兰芝的哥哥　　　　B. 刘兰芝的母亲
    C. 焦仲卿的妹妹　　　　D. 焦仲卿的母亲

5. 刘兰芝离开焦仲卿家后,去了哪里?（　　）

    A. 焦仲卿的妹妹家　　　B. 刘兰芝的哥哥家
    C. 刘兰芝的妹妹家　　　D. 焦仲卿的姐姐家

6. 刘兰芝的母亲看见刘兰芝被送回刘家,她的心情是什么样的?（　　）

    A. 很不高兴　B. 很开心　　C. 很害怕　　D. 很感动

7. 太守想让刘兰芝嫁给自己的第几个儿子?（　　）

    A. 一　　　　B. 三　　　　C. 五　　　　D. 七

8. 刘兰芝的哥哥听说刘兰芝不想嫁给太守的儿子,他的心情是什么样的?(　　)

A. 很不高兴　B. 很开心　C. 很害怕　D. 很感动

9. 焦仲卿后来怎么样了?(　　)

A. 跟刘兰芝跑了　　　　B. 跟刘兰芝一起回家了

C. 跳水塘死了　　　　　D. 上吊了

10. 刘兰芝后来怎么样了?(　　)

A. 跟焦仲卿跑了　　　　B. 跟焦仲卿一起回家了

C. 跳水塘死了　　　　　D. 上吊了

二、判断题:请根据故事内容判断下列说法是否正确,如果正确请标"T",不正确请标"F"。
Decide whether the following statements are true (T) or false (F).

1. 刘兰芝不只漂亮可爱,还很有才能。　　　　(　　)

2. 刘兰芝十几岁就学会了音乐。　　　　　　　(　　)

3. 焦仲卿的母亲很喜欢刘兰芝。　　　　　　　(　　)

4. 刘兰芝的哥哥想让刘兰芝等着焦仲卿来接她。(　　)

5. 太守送了刘兰芝的家人很多礼物。　　　　　(　　)

6. 刘兰芝爱焦仲卿,也爱太守的儿子。　　　　(　　)

7. 刘兰芝要嫁给太守的儿子了,她非常开心。　(　　)

8. 焦仲卿和刘兰芝一起跳水塘死了。　　　（　　）

9. 焦仲卿和刘兰芝死后,他们的家人才明白他们爱得有多深。

（　　）

10. 焦仲卿和刘兰芝的墓地旁有两只猫。　　（　　）

三、选择填空。 Choose the appropriate words to fill in the parentheses.

1. 时间像水一样一天天过去,刘兰芝也从一个小女孩儿长成了(　　)。这时的刘兰芝不只漂亮可爱,还非常有(　　)。她在十三四岁时就学会了自己动手做(　　)。在她十五岁时,父母找人教她学习(　　),她学得很认真。十六岁时,她读(　　)就已经读得很好了,连她的(　　)都比不过她。

A. 音乐　　B. 衣服　　C. 才能　　D. 哥哥
E. 少女　　F. 书

2. 房间里(　　)他一个人,但是他记得自己和妻子在一起所有的(　　)。他记得她第一次来到自己家时,像小孩子一样(　　);他记得她一边做家务一边笑得很(　　);他记得她一边跟他说话,一边把自己打扮得像画里的美人儿一样……他们曾经那么(　　)地生活在一起,最后却还是不得不分开。想到这里,他又一次(　　)了起来。

A. 哭　　　B. 只有　　　C. 快乐　　　D. 高兴

E. 开心　　F. 幸福

3. 月亮（　　）了，晚上到来了，人们都准备（　　）了。刘兰芝一个人（　　）了院子里的水塘旁边，她在那里（　　）了一会儿，（　　）旁边没有人，便一下子（　　）了下去。

A. 来到　　B. 休息　　C. 坐　　　D. 跳

E. 出来　　F. 见

四、连线题。 Match.

1. 请为下列词语选择合适的搭配。

A. 娶　　　　　　a. 书

B. 生　　　　　　b. 家务

C. 做　　　　　　c. 妻子

D. 种　　　　　　d. 孩子

E. 读　　　　　　e. 树

2. 根据故事内容为下列事物选择各自的特征。

A. 个子　　　　　a. 短暂的

B. 心眼儿　　　　b. 好

C. 小鸟　　　　　c. 高

D. 爱　　　　　　d. 可爱的

E. 生命　　　　　e. 永恒的

五、请根据故事内容给下列句子排列顺序。
Put the following statements in order according to the story.

A. 焦仲卿把刘兰芝送回了刘兰芝哥哥家。

B. 焦仲卿的母亲越来越不喜欢刘兰芝，就想把她赶走。

C. 焦仲卿在院子里的大树下走来走去，随后在树上上吊了。

D. 刘兰芝在十七岁这一年嫁给了焦仲卿，成了他的妻子。

E. 刘兰芝的哥哥收了太守送来的礼物，要把刘兰芝嫁给太守的第五个儿子。

F. 焦仲卿骑马去了刘兰芝哥哥家，与刘兰芝约好一起去死。

G. 刘兰芝一个人来到了院子里的水塘旁边，一下子跳了下去。

六、图片题。Answer the following questions according to the picture.

1. 请根据图片说说这幅图应该放在这本书的第（　　　）页。

2. 图中的人物是谁？

3. 图中的人物心情怎么样？

4. 图中人物的心情为什么会是这样的？

5. 请你用中文或英文给这幅图加一个简单的标题说明。

练习题答案 Keys to the exercises

一、选择题
1. B   2. C   3. C   4. D   5. B
6. A   7. C   8. A   9. D   10. C

二、判断题：请根据故事内容判断下列说法是否正确，如果正确请标"T"，不正确请标"F"
1. T   2. T   3. F   4. F   5. T
6. F   7. F   8. F   9. T   10. F

三、选择填空
1. E   C   B   A   F   D
2. B   C   D   E   F   A
3. E   B   A   C   F   D

四、连线题
1. A-c, B-d, C-b, D-e, E-a   2. A-c, B-b, C-d, D-e, E-a

五、请根据故事内容给下列句子排列顺序
D-B-A-E-F-G-C

词汇表
Vocabulary List

笨	adj.	bèn	stupid
不孝	v.	búxiào	be unfilial
曾经	adv.	céngjīng	once
打扮	v.	dǎban	dress up
到底	adv.	dàodǐ	on earth
短暂	adj.	duǎnzàn	brief, transient
夫妻	n.	fūqī	husband and wife, couple
赶	v.	gǎn	drive away
怪	v.	guài	blame
官员	n.	guānyuán	official
规矩	n.	guīju	(good) manners
害怕	v.	hàipà	fear
合葬	v.	hézàng	bury in one grave
嫁	v.	jià	(of women) marry
健康	adj.	jiànkāng	healthy
接	v.	jiē	pick up
礼物	n.	lǐwù	gift
邻居	n.	línjū	neighbor
媒人	n.	méiren	matchmaker
墓地	n.	mùdì	grave
脾气	n.	píqi	temper
骑	v.	qí	ride
强迫	v.	qiǎngpò	force, compel
娶	v.	qǔ	(of men) marry
劝	v.	quàn	persuade
山珍海味	idiom	shānzhēnhǎiwèi	delicacies of every kind
上吊	v.	shàngèdiào	hang oneself
深	adj.	shēn	deep
失去	v.	shīqù	lose
水塘	n.	shuǐtáng	pool
死亡	v.	sǐwáng	death
太守	n.	tàishǒu	prefect, a position in ancient China equivalent to current provincial governor.
小鸟	n.	xiǎo niǎo	little bird
心愿	n.	xīnyuàn	wish
休	v.	xiū	divorce (one's wife)
意义	n.	yìyì	meaning
永恒	adj.	yǒnghéng	eternal
有钱有势		yǒu qián yǒu shì	rich and powerful
院子	n.	yuànzi	courtyard
祝贺	v.	zhùhè	congratulate

项目策划：刘小琳　韩　颖
责任编辑：刘小琳
英文编辑：薛彧威
英文翻译：韩芙芸
英文审订：黄长奇
设计指导：isles studio
设计制作：isles studio

图书在版编目（CIP）数据

焦仲卿与刘兰芝：汉、英 / 刘菊改编．— 北京：华语教学出版社，2016
（"彩虹桥"汉语分级读物．2级：500词）
ISBN 978-7-5138-0976-4

Ⅰ．①焦… Ⅱ．①刘… Ⅲ．①汉语－对外汉语教学－语言读物 Ⅳ．① H195.5

中国版本图书馆 CIP 数据核字（2015）第 155707 号

焦仲卿与刘兰芝

刘　菊　改编

*

©华语教学出版社有限责任公司
华语教学出版社有限责任公司出版
（中国北京百万庄大街24号　邮政编码 100037）
电话：(86)10-68320585　68997826
传真：(86)10-68997826　68326333
网址：www.sinolingua.com.cn
电子信箱：hyjx@sinolingua.com.cn
北京京华虎彩印刷有限公司印刷
2016年（32开）第1版
2019年第1版第3次印刷
（汉英）
ISBN 978-7-5138-0976-4
定价：22.00元